Legal Disclaimer

The author of this book is not an attorney and makes no claim to be one. The information in this book does not create or constitute a client relationship. The materials presented in this book are based solely on the experiences of the author.

Table of Contents

FORWARD

I want to thank you very much for purchasing **MS Word Legal -- *Awareness Explosion* Volume 4**. This book represents another hefty amount of articles that vastly increase your MS Word knowledge base. The insight you get from simply reading the material is amazing! If you purchase any of the four volume set, you gain a tremendous amount of insight,

Do you want to save hundreds of hours of time waiting for scenarios to happen in order to learn valuable lessons or do you hope to get the information from some huge technical book? We have already been through the scenarios and you will certainly appreciate the effort. This book gives you a window into working in a top-tier legal word processing center. I promise that this book goes over a tremendous amount of material that you will be the beneficiary of.

After looking at the articles produced as a whole, I realized, that so much ground has been covered that I saw the need to release it to the public. This book can be used as a study guide for people trying to get into the legal business, to increase the awareness of those working within a legal environment and to give others such as job agency people and those working for single practitioners and smaller offices, a good feel of the day to day interactions and subject matter encountered within a large law firm.

I write the articles I do because I see too much generic talk and wanted to make sure that people deal with and see what really goes on from day to day the good and sometimes stressful. Think of this series as a great expansion of your knowledge base. Feel free to follow me on LinkedIn at the Group AdvanceTo Legal and Corporate Word Processing Training Forum. My email is louis@advanceto.com. The website is advanceto.com. Through that site you can contact us for basic-advanced Legal MS Word Training. We do public training as well as transforming legal firms large and small with our style of training.

Best regards,

Louis

TO CROSS REFERENCE OR NOT CROSS REFERENCE...
THAT IS THE QUESTION

This article is a strategic article based on certain circumstances. Thank you student Deborah for bringing this up.

SCENARIO:

Section 2.01 The Contract (Style Separator) Body Text Body Text Body Text Body Text Body Text Body Text Body Text **See Section 5.04 and 5.05** for the provisions allowing third party intervention.

1. So, above, we have a Heading 2. This Heading 2 has the word Section as part of the "Numbering Aspect" of Heading 2. Therefore, each time we cross reference to a Heading 2 paragraph, the word "Section" will be included in the Field Code.

2. In the example above, when I do the cross reference to Section 5.04, I will get a Gray Field Code that says Section 5.04 since the word "Section" is part of the numbering system in the Multilevel Dialog box. If it were not, then I would have to type in the word "Section" (regular text) since I would only get a Field Code that says 5.04. With me so far?

3. So, in my example above, it says "**See Section 5.04 and 5.05**". Note that the reference to 5.05 does NOT have the word "Section" before it. This was the intention of the attorney who authored the document. The question then becomes whether to cross reference the 5.05 which will give us the word Section or to leave it "**as is**" meaning as just text.

4.   While some might be tempted to leave it as plain text, it is very easy to alter the Field Code for the reference to 5.05.

5.   Bring in the cross reference for 5.05 and you will get the usual Section 5.05. Right click on the field code and choose Edit Field. On the right side of the large dialog box, check the box that reads "**Suppress All Non-Delimitor Chars**". This will suppress the word "**Section**" for that reference only.

6.   Now, you do not have to sacrifice not using your cross reference function simply because a particular instance was different.

*   *   *
... ...

FOLLOW NUMBER WITH NOTHING?

WHAT IS THIS ABOUT?

HERE IS THE SCENARIO:

You have the following Heading Centered on your page

ARTICLE I (Soft Return)
INTRODUCTION (Hard Return)

1   In the Multilevel Outline Dialog Box, the Word "Article" and the automated number I (Roman) are all considered part of the **numbering aspect** for this level Heading 1.

2.   In the Multilevel Outline Dialog Box, there is an area called "**Follow Number With**". Normally, when the Numbering part of the Heading **Shares** the line with the Textual part of the Heading, we use Follow Number with "Tab".

3.   In our scenario above, the **Numbering Aspect** of the Heading resides on the line **by itself**. Therefore, in this scenario we choose Follow Number With "**Nothing**". This is because there is nothing following the numbering aspect of the Heading as shown in the example above.

4.   If you do happen to use Follow Number With "**Tab**" in this scenario, you would lose points on a hands-on test, cause the centered Heading to be slightly off center and in a law firm environment, your co-workers would notice it as well. Now that you are aware of this type of situation, you will now be less likely to make the error.

TWO SCENARIOS BUT ONE HEADING TO COVER THEM BOTH

This particular question has come up a number of times so it is best to clarify and remove the confusion associated with it.

HERE IT IS:

You have a Heading Level 2. In some instances within the document the Heading 2 sits by itself. For example:

Section 2.01 The Time Frame.

In the scenario above, Heading 2 resides by itself.

Let's now look at the scenario below:

Section 2.02. The Management.(Style Separator) Blah blah blah blah blah blah blah blah blah blah blah blah blah blah blah blah blah blah blah blah blah blah blah blah blah blah blah blah blah blah blah blah blah blah blah blah blah blah blah blah blah blah blah blah blah blah blah blah blah blah blah blah blah blah blah blah blah.

In the above example, Heading 2 shares the paragraph and therefore will need the use of the Style Separator. After the Heading 2 text (after the Style Separator), a Body Text is applied to the remainder of the paragraph in order to disassociate that text from the Heading 2 so it does not end up in the TOC.

So the question arises, do I need to have a separate Heading Level in order to accommodate a Heading 2 type heading that resides by itself vs a Heading 2 type heading that shares the paragraph? The answer is **NO**. Heading 2 takes care of both scenarios and the sequential numbering system of Heading 2 is **not affected** whether the Heading is by itself or Sharing the paragraph. The numbering will continue to tally properly.

......*

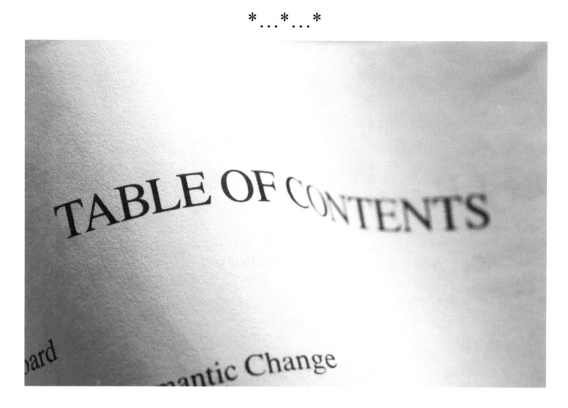

TABLE OF CONTENTS, HEADINGS AND TITLES

As you know, or may not know, most Table of Contents are based off of the Heading Styles. Some TOC"s are a combination of Headings and Titles.

But, sometimes the Heading Styles are used in a way whereby they don't qualify as Headings in the sense of what would traditionally appear in a Table of Contents.

Let me give you an example:

Introduction (Style Name-Title Center)

(STYLE - HEADING 1)

1.　The basis for this Agreement stems from the negotiations that took place over a four day period during the week of September 21.

2　The Agreement which will define how Company A will merge with Company B will be fully examined within this document.　The following will be discussed:

(STYLE - HEADING 2)

(a)　The time frame involved blah blah blah.

(b)　The Management of the company blah blah blah.

(c)　Duplication of the Staff will be examined blah blah blah.

So in the example above, the Headings are really not useful to the TOC so therefore I would be looking at the Titles of the document.

When you open up the TOC Dialog Box and go to Options, you would look for the Title Styles that you want to use within your TOC and place a number 1 or 2 next to the style name.　The numbers represent the **SLOT** that the TOC level will occupy when run.

......*

In this scenario, since you won't be using the Headings, make sure you remove **ANY** numbers next to the Heading 1 and Heading 2 under Options so that they will be excluded from the TOC.

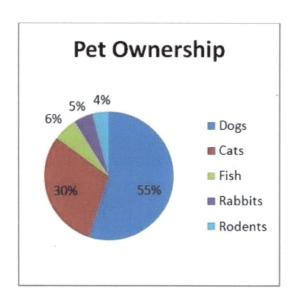

THE DIFFERENCE BETWEEN DATA SERIES AND DATA LABELS:

This subject has to do with PowerPoint Items Found in Pie, Charts, Bar Graphs, Line Charts etc.

Let's use a Pie Chart as a good Visual to define Data Label Vs. Data Series.

Scenario Our Pie Chart Involves the Percentage of those people in certain groups that have a Pet. The Groups are 1. Business Owners, 2. Office Workers, 3. Blue Collar Workers, 4. IT Professionals and 5. Retired Workers.

1.   For this scenario, let us assume that the percentages of the different categories of workers went as follows: Business Owners 20%, Office Workers 30%, Blue collar 25%, IT Pros 0.5% and Retired 20%.

2.   Picture the Slices of the pie and on each slice of the pie, picture the size of each slice based on the percentage of each category type that owns a pet.

3.   The Percentage figures that you see on each individually colored slice of the pie are known as **Data Labels**.

4   The **Data Series** would be the different categories of people that were polled in order to produce the chart as a whole. In this case, the Data Series would be composed of **5 separate categories** (each a Data Label), producing the 5 slice pie.

5.	Each individual part of the Data Series (each part of the pie) can be formatted individually in terms of color, while each individual Data Label (the percentages) can be formatted in terms of color and font size.

6.	When you deal with Bar Charts they too have Data Labels on each part of the Bar For Each Separate category.

7.	For each separate **Plot Point** of a Line Chart you can have a Data Label showing at that point. Each Separate category in a Bar Chart and Line Chart is known as an individual Data Series since unlike a Pie Chart, Bar and Line Charts can be composed of multiple Data Series.

......*

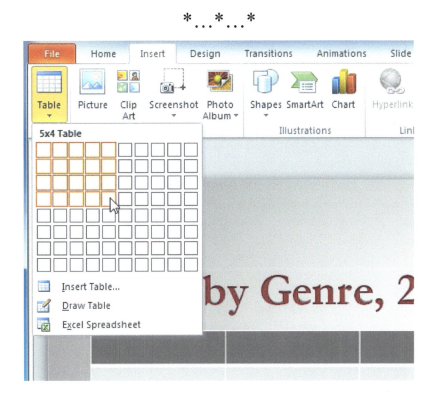

DOING TABLES IN POWERPOINT

TABLES IN POWERPOINT IS A LIGHT VERSION OF MS WORD TABLES.

1.	In MS Word Tables, I can use my Paint Brush for copying attributes and Tab Formatting. In PowerPoint, I can make use of the Paint Brush but it will not work to copy Tab Settings.

2.	Whether I use a Right Tab in the ruler for my Dollar Sign Lines and a Decimal Tab for my Non-Dollar Sign Lines, I still have to do "**Control Tab**" to get to the Decimal Align under PowerPoint. In MS Word Tables, once you set a Decimal Align Tab, the cursor jumps right to the position of where you will type your first number and the number goes in from Right to Left.

3.   **Dotted Leader on the Side Headings Portion in PowerPoint Tables**. To get a Dotted Leader Stemming from each side Heading, you set a Right Tab on the Ruler and under the Home Tab, go to Font and under Underline Type, choose the Dotted Line Type. Now go to the end of line that needs the Dotted Leader and use Control Tab to jump over to the Right Tab you set in the Ruler. In MS Word this would have simply been taken care of with the Tab Setting Dialog Box by choosing selection No. 2 under Leader.

4.   Finally, because you cannot seem to Paint Tabs from one cell to another within PowerPoint Tables there is a crude way to cut down on some of the grunt work of setting Tabs line by line. If you set up your Table in PowerPoint, and have, let us say the next five rows of a specific column that are using a specific tab type **the trick is to create the new rows as you go along**. After you type each line, press your Tab Key to force the creation of a new row. Because it feeds off the prior row, it "**RETAINS**" the tab settings you were using in the cells of the prior row.

Play around with PowerPoint when you can to become comfortable with PowerPoint Tables.

SHOWING PERCENTAGES IN PIE CHARTS, BAR CHARTS AND LINE CHARTS IN POWERPOINT

This subject comes up whether you are doing a Pie Chart, a Bar Chart or a Line Chart. There is a good chance that the data on the Chart will be broken down in percentages.

For example, the percentage of lawyers to paralegal to non legal staff. Another example would be the percentage of 14 year olds with Cell Phones.

PIE CHARTS:

When we do Pie Charts, we can turn our Data Labels on each slice of the Pie to Percentages (For Example 20%, 40%).

So, in order to show percentages in Pie Charts do the following:

1.   Clicking on one Data Label will select all the Data Labels on the Pie Chart.

2.   Right Click and go to Format Data Labels.

3.   Under Label Options, instead of the selection Value, which will show only a number such as "40" instead of 40% choose "Percentage" which will now place the Percentage Symbol" next to each Data Amount (Data Label) on each piece of the Pie.

USE OF PERCENTAGE ON BAR AND LINE CHARTS:

When doing Bar Charts and Line Charts the "**Percentage**" selection is not available so we need to customize the Data Labels in Order to have them show as a Percentage.

So, if we have values in our Bar or Line Chart such as 20, 40, 60 etc. and wish to change them to read as a Percentage, you would do the following:

1.   Click on a Particular Data Series and "ALL" Data Values will now be selected in that Series.

2.   Right click and choose "Format Data Labels".

3.   Go to "Number" and go to "Custom".

4.   Under "Format Code" put in ##\% followed by pressing the "Add" button.

5.   The Data in that Particular Data Series will now show the number as a percentage. (40%)

6.   If the number is initially using a decimal such as 12.4, 2.6, 10.2 then use ##.#\%.

......*

WHEN THE BUFFER COLUMN IS NEEDED IN FINANCIAL TABLES

In this particular article, I will discuss two scenarios where Buffer Columns are used and why vs. when it is not necessary.

COLUMN HEADINGS:

1.   For Column Headings: if you use Border "**Applied To Paragraph**" then this leaves a bit of space on the left and right of the Table Cell and therefore there is no need for a buffer column.   There will be a clear distinction between the two side by side headings.

2.   A buffer column in this case, would "**ONLY**" be used if "**Border Applied To Cell**", were used since "**Border Applied To Cell**" leaves no space within the cell. Two side by side cells using this method will appear as one solid line not two therefore a buffer column would be necessary to produce the visual separation.

USE OF TABLE BORDERS AS SIGNATURE LINES

1   In this scenario, let us suppose we are using the Borders of the table in order to produce the Signature Lines. If the Borders are used, they will stem from end to end and these signature line types placed side by side (two column table) will appear as one long uninterrupted line.

2.   In order to get around this, you need to insert a Buffer Column which you can squeeze down to one character width placed between the two columns. This empty column with no border lines, will serve to create the necessary visual separation so that two side by side signatures using the Table Border method will view as two distinct signature lines.

3.   Finally, if you make use of a right tab in the ruler with a "Solid Line Leader" attached to the Tab to create your signature lines then no buffer would be necessary. These signature line types do not go from end to end.

Try them all and view the difference.

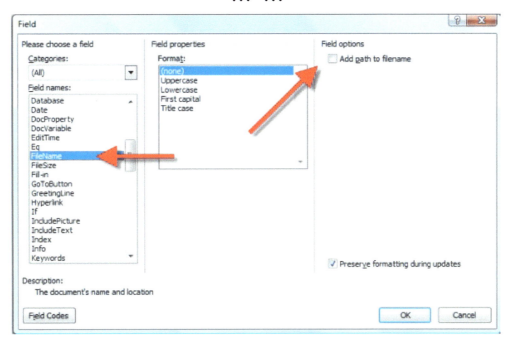

ADDING THE FILE NAME PATH TO YOUR DOC

A little thing that can cause a problem if you have not been exposed to it.

SCENARIO:

You go to an agency to take a test. Within the test instructions, they ask you to place the "Path To Filename" within the Footer of the first page (Cover Page).

Since that would be one of the first things to be done within the test, you don't want to start out by being stumped.

Let's go through the simple routine:

1. Go to Insert and look for Quick Parts on the right side of the ribbon.

2. Look for Field and go into the "Field" dialog box.

3. Look for Filename and select it.

4. Upon doing so, under "Field Options" on the right side of the Dialog Box click on the "Add Path To Filename" button.

5. This will bring in the entire Path of the current document in the same manner that Document Management Systems track a particular file.

......*

IN 2013

BRINGING THE FOOTNOTE TEXT IN FROM ANOTHER DOCUMENT...

When dealing with Footnotes, problems occur when we don't adhere to the basics of how Footnotes are composed. The following is a good reminder of just what controls the Footnotes.

1.   When you insert a Footnote, you end up with a Footnote Reference Number within the body of the text which appears Superscripted as well as a corresponding Reference Number at the bottom of the page associated with the new footnote.

2.   If you sweep your cursor over the Footnote Reference Number "within the text" and look at your Style Pane, it reads "Footnote Reference". Keep in mind that this is a character style "a" and is not a paragraph style. Therefore, you can modify its font characteristics and attributes if needed. This is the name of the style that is associated with the footnote number or symbol. Note: You can also use your Apply Style Toolbar (Control Shift S) to immediately see the Style Associated with the the location of the cursor.

3.   Switch to Print Layout and run your cursor over the Footnote Reference Number next to the actual footnote text (at the bottom of your page) the style associated with the Footnote Number is again "**Footnote Reference**". Now highlight the text of the Footnote Itself and look at your Style Pane. The associated style is called "**Footnote Text**".

4.   This pattern of **Footnote Text** and **Footnote Reference** should not be disturbed.

5.   Finally, to bring Footnote Text in from another location, you would 1) under your Reference tab "Insert Footnote", 2) The Footnote area opens at the bottom awaiting your Footnote Text, 3) Go to the location of the Footnote Text and copy it, 4) Go back to the awaiting open Footnote and paste it in using Paste, Paste Special and choose Unformatted Text, 5) The Footnote text shakes loose the formatting from the original location and *pours* into the "**Footnote Text style**" waiting in the open Footnote.

......*

PAGE NUMBERING PROBLEMS AND DIFFERENT FIRST PAGE:

1.   Each class I teach involves the use of "Different First Page".

2.   Different First Page is found under the "Page Layout Tab" (2007-13) and (Layout Tab) 2016. Within the Page Layout Tab, go to "Page Set-up" and the Layout Tab under Page Set-up. This is where you will see the "Different First Page Selection". You can also find Different First Page under the Header/Footer Ribbon.

3.   "Different First Page" allows you to either 1) Hold off a page number from the first page of a particular Section but bring forth the numbering on the Second Page of that Section and/or 2) place text on the first page of a Section such as DRAFT but NOT continue that same text from the second page forward of that same section. That is the job of Different First Page.

4.   Without Different First Page, attempting to exclude the page number from page 1, the page number will show up on Page 1 regardless.

5.   Having trouble with Page Numbering is usually a combination of Different First Page and forgetting to take off Link To Previous. Forgetting to take off Link To Previous results in unwanted page numbering in certain sections of your document.

SO, TO SET THE PAGE NUMBERING ON THE MAIN PART OF THE DOCUMENT.

      A.   Make sure Different First Page is active for the Entire Document.

      B.   Select Insert Footer, and Choose Edit Footer

      C.   When the Footer area opens up, immediately turn off Link To Previous.

      D.   Go to the Page Number Button (3rd Button From Left) and go to Format Page Numbers.

      E.   Select the 1,2,3 style and choose Start at 1. Select OK to exit the Dialog Box.

      F.   Go Straight to the bottom of Page 2. Remove Link To Previous, Center the Cursor (Control E).

      G.   Go into your Page Number Button (3rd Button From Left) and choose "Current Location" and make the Selection "Plain Number".

      H.   Your number will come in on Page 2 as 2 and you are now set for the remainder of that Section no matter how long the section is.

......*

REMOVING MY CONTINUOUS SECTION BREAKS RESULTS IN DESTROYING MY NEXT PAGE SECTION BREAKS

A lot of you will appreciate this particular write-up. At one time or another, you have had this happen. I don't believe this is a basic or advanced thing. This is just one of the many things that can drive you crazy.

Scenario: You run an Index of Terms and realize that you have placed your cursor in the wrong location and now you have an Index of Terms in an unintended location. You already had saved the document, so you can't undo it. As you know, a completed Index of Terms is surrounded by two "**Continuous Section Breaks**".

Note: Normally, if the Index of Terms is generated in the proper place, the Continuous Breaks cause No Harm. Now the fun begins.

1.   As you attempt to remove the Continuous Section Breaks they then eat up the previous "**Next Page**" type Section Break and before you know it, all of your Next Page type Section Breaks are being replaced with Continuous Breaks and destroying the numbering structure of the document as well as other effects that you don't need.

2.   If this happens on a test, it can throw you off your game and result in a lower score. If this happens at your job, you waste time attempting to put the structure of the document back together.

3.   If this should happen, highlight a few lines before the offending area (Continuous Section Break) as well the Continuous Break under the Index as well.

4.   Go to the Page Layout Tab (Layout Tab in 2016) and under Page Setup - Layout - Next to "Section Start" choose the "New Page" selection. This will change the **Continuous Section Break** to a **New Page** Section Break.

5. Then, just delete the unnecessary Index and go position yourself at the correct location and simply re-run the Index of Terms.

6. It will now come in surrounded by two Continuous Section Breaks which is proper and you will now be back in business.

......*

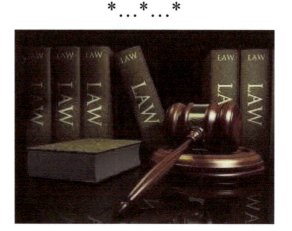

STATUTES, RULES AND TABLE OF AUTHORITIES

All of my students receive a thorough Table of Authorities Litigation class. When they are done, they are very good at setting up simple and complex Caption Boxes as well as a concise Table of Authorities page composed of **Cases**, **Statutes** and **Rules**.

When doing a Table of Authorities, a lot of my new students are confused when it comes to recognizing Federal Statutes vs. State related Statutes. The link below, will help you to see the pattern of the Federal Statutes and the State Statutes State by State. All fifty states are covered in the link below.

https://www.law.cornell.edu/citation/3-300

While Statutes pertain to the law, Rules (Federal or State) pertain to the workings and rules of the particular court the case is being heard in. Federal courts and State Courts have rules that govern every aspect of the chronology of a court case. How long do I have to respond to a Motion, what documents are submitted after the initial complaint? How long do we have to answer the Complaint and on and on.

Below is a link that will discuss the Federal Rules vs. the Rules of the various State Court systems.

https://law.duke.edu/lib/researchguides/courtr/

If you get comfortable with the subject of Statutes and Rules then the remainder of doing a Table of Authorities is quite simple and each separate category of Authorities is easy to designate and separate in the Table of Authorities Dialog Box.

If you need our 4.5 hour class on Table of Authorities, simply contact us at 888-422-0692.

$$*\ldots*\ldots*$$

The Difference Between Defined Terms and Definitions

This article will clarify the difference between (**"Defined Terms"**) and the **"Definitions"** section of an Agreement or other similar document.

AS TO DEFINED TERMS. ("DEFINED TERMS")

1.   The Index of Defined Terms always sits after the Table of Authorities (if you have one) or after the Table of Contents if you do not have a Table of Authorities in a particular document.

2.   Defined terms are designed to allow the author of a document to refer to a company, entity, individual, etc. in a **shortened** manner. So, if we have for example **The New York Board of Education** referred to numerous times throughout the document, you would most probably see this organization name defined in the following way: The New York Board of Education ("NYBOE"). Once the entity has been defined after the first use of the full entity name, you can then refer to that entity with the shortened term "NYBOE" for the remainder of the document.

3.   When the defined terms are marked (References Tab) and an Index of Defined Terms is generated, the reader then has a list of all the terms in the document that were defined and the page number showing where the full version of the term was mentioned.

THE DEFINITIONS SECTION:

1   This usually comes in as one of the first sections of the document. Depending on the size and complexity of the document, you can have a short or a substantial Definitions section.

A TYPICAL DEFINITION:

The Bank. For the purposes of this document, the term Bank will refer specially to Barclay's Bank of London.

1.   The key words above are "For the purposes of this document"...

2   The definitions clarify the use of a particular term within the context of the current document. Outside of the document that same term can have a wholly different meaning.

3.   Unlike the ("Defined Term")

No need to mark or generate anything. Definitions just serve to clarify the meaning of a term within the context of the current document.

......*

WHEN APPLYING STYLES - PLACE THE STYLE YOU ARE APPLYING MOST ON THE CLIPBOARD....

Scenario: Styles are applied to a large file. You have **Heading Styles** for the **Multilevel Outline**, **Body Text Styles** for the non-numbered paragraphs, and a **Style Separator** scenario whereby the text to the right of the Style Separator uses a **Body Text** type style to **disassociate** the remaining Body Text from the Heading 2 text that sits before the Style Separator.

When putting together an involved document, you don't want to have to go up and down the right side style pallet looking for each needed style. That eats up a lot of time and results in a lot of unnecessary movement. Instead, we use a combination of things in order to smooth out the process of applying styles.

BACK TO YOUR STYLE SEPARATOR EXAMPLE:

1.   You have the right side palette open where you are staring at Heading 2.

2.   After we bring in the first instance of the Body Text style that is applied after the Style Separator, we can place the formatting of that style we will use again and again on your "**clip board**" by the use of **Control Shift C**. This style will now be available all day as needed on your clipboard until of course you establish a new **Control Shift C**.

3.   The sequence then becomes apply the Heading 2 Style to the text that shares the paragraph. Heading 2 and its attributes come in.

4.   Apply the Style Separator (Control Alt Enter) and your cursor will be sitting to the right of the Style Separator.

5.   Use **Control Shift V** to paste the formatting of the body text style you placed on the clipboard that disassociates the Body Text from the Heading 2 text.

6.   This method will help to cut down on much of the movement associated with applying styles. The use of the **Control Shift V** is more **efficient** than using the **Paint Brush**. FYI: Control Shift C and Control Shift V is the key combination for the Perpetual use Paint Brush meaning the Paint Brush that was **double clicked**.

7.   Placing your most used style on the clipboard for your editing session will make the process of applying styles a lot easier.

……*

TWO SEPARATE FONT AREAS TO DEAL WITH

Many of us use 3rd Party Software for our Multilevel Outlines. Some of us, on the other hand, use the generic MS Word Multilevel Outline feature. It works well, but people do forget to take care of both Font areas. They are the Font areas controlling the **Numbering** and **Textual Aspect** of each Heading Level.

It is common to forget to take care of the Font that controls the Numbering Aspect. This results in the Numbering text having a different look from the remainder of the particular Heading.

Another scenario that occurs because the Numbering Font was not checked, is the Invisible Level Number problem. Below, I take you through that scenario.

THE INVISIBLE ARTICLE 1

SCENARIO: LEVEL HEADING 1 CENTERED

Article 1 (soft return)

Introduction (Hard Return) (12 Pts. After)

When Heading 1 was set up using the Multi-Level Outline Dialog Box using the configuration "Article 1" as the Numbering Aspect, the following occurred:

1. After implementing Heading 1, it came in in the following manner:

Introduction (Hard Return)

↵
Introduction¶

1.   There was an empty soft return followed by the textual aspect of Heading 1. The numbering aspect DID NOT come in.

2.   Thinking we have overlooked something in the Multi-Level Dialog Box we went back in.   Article 1 was in place and we checked that Level 1 was in fact "Linked" to Heading 1.

3.   Going back to the Heading 1 text in the actual document, we stripped it back to Normal style (**Control Shift N**).   We reapplied Heading 1 and again, it came in with an empty soft return and the textual aspect of Heading 1.

4.   Going back to the Multi-Level Dialog Box we went into the **Font Button** and the CULPRIT was staring at us. Under Font Color, it read "**No Color**". We switched it to "**Automatic**" and Article 1 was now visible. Problem solved.

5.   Remember to deal with both the **Numbering Aspect Font** and the **Textual Aspect Font** of each individual level Heading you implement.

......*

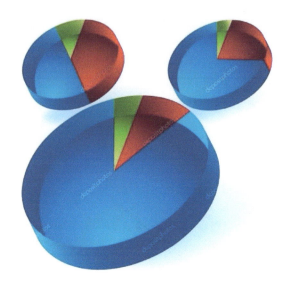

PIE CHARTS IN 3D

1 After you bring in your Pie Chart, clicking on one slice will select all the slices of the chart. A second click on that **same** slice, will now leave only "that particular slice" selected which means "that" particular slice would be affected by any change you make.

2. Back to our "fully" selected Pie Chart. To enhance the look so that the chart is not a 2 dimensional flat figure, go to your Home Tab and over to "**Quick Styles**".

3. Under **Quick Styles**, you have **Light Outline**, **Subtle Effect**, **Moderate Effect**, **Intense Effect**. As you go up the ladder, the more depth the slices will have, meaning the more 3D it will look.

4. You can match any color of your Pie Chart with the effects in Quick Styles, and once you do, your Legend will reflect the new color effect and look.

5. Depending on the color of your **Data Labels**, you can alter the color, by selecting the Data Labels and going to Font and/or you can apply a "**Shape Fill**" color to the Data Label which will create a different look to the Data Labels which works for certain Pie Charts.

6. Finally, for Pie Charts that are uniform in color: Besides showing **Data Labels** sometimes showing "**Category Names**" on the Slices helps as well. To do so, Select your Data Labels, right click and go down to "**Format Data Labels**" and down to "**Category Name**" and place a check next to the selection. When you are back to the Pie Chart, readjust the Font size so that the "Category Name" and "Data Label" comfortably fit on the slice.

……*

HAVING IT BOTH WAYS: PRESET VS. HARD CODED

THIS ARTICLE IS ABOUT A SIMPLE FIX TO A COMMON PROBLEM.

Scenario: Secretary generates a Table of Contents. On the completed TOC, the page numbers are displaying with dashes on either side of the number. -1- The attorney says although he wanted the page numbers within the document to display with the dashes on either side, he does not wish to carry that look over to the page numbers of the completed Table of Contents.

1   When the secretary inserted the page number field code, a "preset" was used (Header/Footer Toolbar, "Page Number Icon"/ Current Position) that in essence, creates a field code that automates the page numbers. The pre-set that was used has built in dashes. Because they are part of the Page Number Field Code, they then are displayed as part of the numbering system of the Table of Contents.

2   What needs to be done is to remove the preset page numbering.

3.   Go back to the Header Footer Tool Bar, over to the Page Number Icon (Left Side)

4.   Under Current Position, choose the first scenario which is the "Plain Text" option.

5.   Once the field code for the Plain Text auto numbering comes in, place a dash on the left and right side of the code such as -1-

6.   Because the dashes are not part of the numbering field code, they will not be included in the page numbering of the completed Table of Contents.

......*

CONTROLLING THE LOOK OF MY INDEX OF TERMS PAGE NUMBERS

This does not come up everyday but when it does, it is good to know how to deal with it. If you don't, a simple thing like this can lose you points on a test and force you to use Direct Formatting unnecessarily. It really is a very simple thing to do but people sometimes do not pick up on where this is taken care of.

Scenario: You are asked to run an Index of Terms whereby the Page Numbers are requested to be Bolded or Italicized. I have seen this scenario with a couple of different twists which I will go over with you.

1. The Page Numbers of the Index of Terms are controlled from the "**Mark Index Entry**" Dialog Box. Within the box, you have an area called "**Page Number Format**". You can choose **Bold**, *Italic* or ***Bold Italic*** (Both)

2. Now that you know how to control the Page Number in terms of attributes, let's run through the scenarios dealing with the generated Index of Terms.

3. If they want the Terms Bolded, Underscored or Italicized only in the text of the document, mark the terms first then apply your attributes. Using a **Character Style** will give you the most control as to modifying or deleting the attribute.

4. Conversely, if you want the Terms to show up with the Bold, Underscore or Italic Attribute in the Generated Index then **apply your attributes first** then mark each term.

5. As to the Page No. Being Bold, Italic or both in your Index: For each term that you mark, if you leave the "Main Index Entry" Dialog Box up and you choose Bold Italic or both, you will NOT have to reselect the Bold or Italic attribute for each individual entry. Just remember that as you highlight each entry click in the "Main Entry Box" (at the top of the Dialog Box) to update the memory concerning the current entry and you will be fine.

* … * … *

STRIPPING A CHARACTER STYLE WON'T AFFECT THE PARAGRAPH STYLE IF DONE CORRECTLY.

I RECENTLY WROTE AN ARTICLE ENTITLED "MARK IT FIRST THEN ADD YOUR ATTRIBUTES".

This article (Thanks Student Robert) had to do with requests for you to run an Index of Terms.

An Index of Terms is a listing of all of the "Shortcuts" used within a document. In the scenario, we are asked to Bold the ("**Defined Terms**") of the document. When I am asked to do so, I use a Character style that does nothing more than Bold the Defined Terms. I was NOT asked to have the Terms Bolded within the Index.

The present article is about Bolding the Defined Terms and then at some point having to fix a few instances of the Bolded Defined Terms.

1.   If I bold a **Defined Term** by using Direct Formatting or by use of a Character Style, followed by marking the Defined Term, the bolding attribute will carry over to your Index of Terms.

2.   If I mark the Defined Term then apply the Bold Attribute, the Bolding **Will Not** carry over to your **Index of Defined Terms**.

3.   If I Bold the Defined Term with a Character Style, I remove the Bolding by going to the Home Tab and clicking off the bold attribute button followed by THEN marking the Defined Term, it will STILL display Bolded in your finished Index. This is so because even though the Bolding attribute was turned off (Manually), the Character Style is still silently attached to that piece of text and will still result in carrying over the Bold Attribute to your Index.

4.   The best way to turn off the character style on 1 or a few instances of text that have been inadvertently formatted with a Character Style or is to highlight the piece of text and use **Control Shift N or Control Spacebar.**

5.   **Control Shift N or Control Spacebar** will strip off the Character Style as well as Control Spacebar without stripping the Paragraph Style the Defined Term is presently sitting in. Then, when you mark the Term you can be assured that the Bolding will not carry over to the Index. Remember: Highlight the piece you are removing the Character Style from.

......*

SETTING A DOCUMENT PASSWORD VS. RESTRICT EDITING

This write-up will be helpful in clarifying the difference between setting a Password for a document so that the recipient cannot open it without the having the password. This is different from making use of "Restrict Formatting and Editing Mode" which allows the recipient to access the document but having restrictions placed on what can be altered. So let us go over both:

PASSWORD PROTECTION:

1.   Go To **File**, **Info** "**Protect Document**" Permissions.

2.   Under the "**Protect Document**" Button, go down to "Encrypt With Password".

3.   Type Your Password. Make sure you write it down somewhere. Also, from experience, make sure your fingers are on the proper place on the keyboard because you can type your "password" in wrong 2x and think you typed it in correctly. Then, when someone tries to open it with your "password", it does not work and you and the recipient are locked out and stressed out. It may also be a great idea to save a unencrypted copy of the file as well before you set the password.

As to "**Restrict Editing**" you can get to it from File, Info, Protect Document, Restrict Editing or you can get to it from the Developer Tab as well as the Review Tab.

......*

1.   With **Restrict Editing**, we use it to lock a document for **Fillable Forms**, as well as allowing certain types of editing and determining groups and/or individuals that can do so.

2.   When doing Fillable Forms, we restrict the document so that the recipient can only type in the form fields while the text of the document is off limits.

I suggest you familiarize yourself with both scenarios discussed in this article.

......*

I WANT MY "STYLE" BOX BACK...

That was the simple request that the Operator made. I want my "**Style**" box back. Not understanding what she meant right off the bat, I asked a series of questions:

1.   Are you talking about your "Style Area Pane" (Draft View) under Format Options, Advanced that Tracks each applied style? The answer was no.

2.   Are you talking about your right side Style Pallet that you turn on under the Home Tab and Styles. The answer was no.

3.   Are you talking about the Apply Styles Toolbar (Control Shift S) which shows you the style your cursor is presently on. The answer again was no. Your Gallery? No, no, no

4.   It always sits in my Quick Access Toolbar and now it is gone. She is referring to the "Style" box. Your Quick Access Toolbar contains things such as Save, Undo, Redo etc. To turn on the "Style" box, do the following:

5.   Go to File, Options, Quick Access Toolbar and on the left side choose "All Commands". Look for the command that says "**Style**".

6.   Choose "**Style**" and Add it to the list on the right side. When you exit back to the regular screen, you will now see your "**Style Box**" sitting in your Quick Access Toolbar.

7.   The style box is a very useful tool to let you know the Style name of the text that your cursor is presently on.

Check it out or install it to your Quick Access Toolbar. This holdover from MS Word 2003 is still very useful.

MARKING STRATEGY FOR TABLE OF AUTHORITIES
AND INDEX OF TERMS

This scenario will come up again and again. You want to know how certain things affect the outcome of your completed Table of Authorities or Index of Terms to better control the outcome. We don't want to manually manipulate the completed TOA or Index of Terms with Direct Formatting because as soon as it is rerun, you will be back to square 1. Let's look at two scenarios

Scenario 1. Attorney wants Defined Terms Bold and/or Underscored. They do not want the **Bold** or <u>Underscore</u> in the completed Index of Terms.

Ans: Mark your Defined Terms **first** followed by applying your **Bold and/or Underscore** attribute using a Character Style. Using the **Character Style**, will give you more control over the attribute because you can remove it and easily reapply the Bold or Underscore through simple Modification.

Scenario 2:

Attorney wants the cases of the Table of Authorities to be Underscored or Italicized within the text but not to be carried over to the TOA.

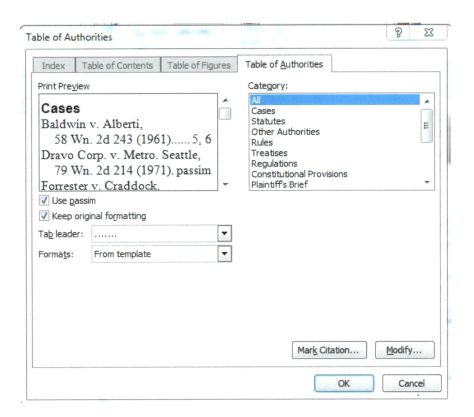

Ans: Mark the Table of Authorities First followed by Underscoring or Italicizing the case name using a Character Style. Even easier: If you Italize or Underscore the case names and you check the box above "Keep Original Formatting" you will get the same attributes in your TOA. Uncheck it and you will just get the text.

Keep this in mind next time you work on a Litigation Document. What does your finished TOA and Index look like and what is the attorney preference in terms of the look of the completed TOA and Index.

......*

INCLUDING TITLES AND HEADINGS IN THE TOC

For many of the styled documents that are done in a typical day, they make use of the Heading Styles in order to create the Table of Contents. The typical TOC is composed of Headings 1 and 2.

Sometimes, we are asked to include "**Title styles**" as part of the TOC. This will involve the "**Options**" area of your TOC Dialog Box. Under the "Reference" button and under Table of Contents, go to "**Insert**" if using 2007-10 and "**Customize**" if using 2013 and above.

1.   In your TOC Dialog Box, go to **Options**. You will by default, typically see a number **1** next to Heading **1** and a **2** next to **Heading 2** if you had asked for a 2 level TOC.

2.   Those numbers refer to slots in terms of how far each level will be pushed in across the page when the TOC is generated. So, a number 1 next to Heading 1 under Options, means it will come in at the first slot which means flat against the left margin while the 2 next to Heading 2 under Options, will mean it is pushed in further than the Heading 1 position as an offset.

3.   So, if the attorney asks for a Title Style(s) to be included in the TOC, then go to Options in your TOC Dialog box and look for the Title Style Name that controls the Title that the attorney wants you to include. All active styles being used in the document will always be listed and accounted for under the Options button in the TOC Dialog Box.

4.   Once you find the **Title Style** that you need to include, place a number **1** next to it which will give it the **first slot position**. Run your Table of Contents and now it will generate a **TOC** composed of **Heading 1**, **Heading 2** and the **Title Style** that was requested to be included.

Give it a try next time you run a TOC.

......*

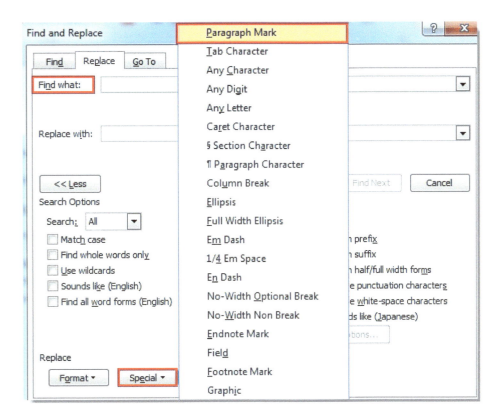

PARAGRAPH MARK VS. PARAGRAPH CHARACTER

Here is the scenario: Client had Adobe reader not the Professional version. They only had an Adobe version of a particular document and they wanted to take the text of that Adobe file and clean it up and style it in MS Word.

1.   The Adobe Document was one that was created from the desktop meaning that it was created while in MS Word and therefore it would be immediately searchable and text accessible.

2.   They selected the text of the PDF file and copied the text over to MS Word bringing it in using paste special and unformatted text.

3.   When the text came in, every line had a hard return that they wanted to get rid of using global replace. I suggested that before they do a wholesale global of the hard returns, they should protect the legitimate ends of the paragraphs so that they can then concentrate on the remainder of the "unnecessary" hard returns that were brought over from the PDF file. With me so far? They might have been better off just scanning the hard copy and saving the scan as a MS Word file then cleaning it up.

4.   In the current scenario, I suggested that they search for . (Period) and hard return and replace that with a character that would stick out and act as a temporary placeholder to represent all instances of "." and hard return (thus, the end of a paragraph). I suggested using the ampersand symbol "&" as the placeholder symbol. Yes, I could

have made use of the "wildcard" feature in MS Word but, I was not sure of exactly how to use it. In fact the wild card would be quicker.

5.　　They tried my suggestion and told me that no replacements were made. They had confused **Paragraph Mark** vs. **Paragraph Character**.　When doing this particular global involving the period and hard return, you go to search and replace and search for . (Period) then you go to special and choose "**Paragraph Mark**"

6.　　Replace with a character such as "**&**" (**ampersand**) which will act as a place holder until you get rid of the extraneous and unnecessary hard returns by searching for hard return (**paragraph mark**) and replacing them with a regular space.

7.　　Finally, when all of your unnecessary hard returns are gone, reverse the first global you did and that will put back your period and hard return at the end of each paragraph.

8.　　Remember, Paragraph Mark refers to a "**return symbol**" or end of the paragraph while Paragraph Character "¶" refers to the actual paragraph symbol that is used in a document as part of a citation).

……*

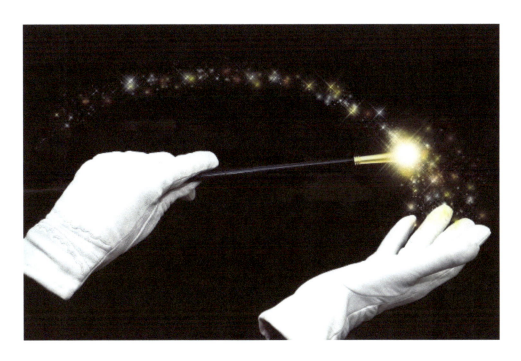

APPLYING STYLES WITH EASE

This short write-up has to do with a situation where you have the need to apply a number of different styles in succession in a particular document and you don't want to hunt up and down the right side style pallet to find the style you need.

JUST TO GO OVER SOME HANDY TOOLS:

1. **Control Shift S** (Apply Styles Toolbar). Type the style name you need and it will pop up in the window and you press your return key to apply the style.

2. **Control Shift C - Control Shift V**. Copy and Paste Formatting. Control Shift C to grab the formatting of a paragraph and Control Shift V to Paste that formatting to another paragraph.

If you have a number of different styles you are using in the document, leave 1 of them on the **Control Shift V** Clipboard. As you need that particular style, place your cursor in the paragraph that needs that particular style applied and press **Control Shift V**. You avoid having to use the **Paint Brush** since **Control Shift V** is equivalent to the **Paint Brush**. It will stay on the clipboard until you introduce another Copy Formatting situation (**Control Shift C**).

3. You can apply a number of successive paragraphs with a style sitting on the Control Shift V clipboard or apply a paragraph with a style on the Control Shift V clipboard and then highlight the next 5 or 10 paragraphs needing that same style and press **F4** for the "**Repeat**" function.

4.   **Double Click** on the Paint Brush while the cursor is sitting in a paragraph of a needed style and "**perpetually**" apply that particular style X number of paragraphs needing that same style.

Using "any" combination of these tools will speed up your applying of styles to large files.

I would suggest you try them all and you will ultimately come up with combinations that make the most sense for you.

......*

VERY SIMPLE, BUT YOU CAN GET MOMENTARILY CONFUSED

I like to include these quick fixes because minor problems are amplified when a person is under time constraint, and is having trouble focusing on the actual problem.

SO HERE IS THE SCENARIO:

Document has a large table mostly consisting of text that extends over 20 pages. It has a large textual header row. The Header Row repeats on each page because "Header Row Repeat" has been selected.

The operator is attempting to edit Header Material and cannot click upon this text to make the edits. They have already spent much time looking at the table thinking someone has locked that part of the document from being able to be edited.

What actually happened is the following:

1.   The attorney, 10 pages into the paper copy (Hard Copy), made edits to the large repeating table heading sitting at the top of the table on page 10.

2.   The operator, being on page 10 of the MS Word document was trying to edit the area that the attorney made edits to no avail.

3.   The operator was then directed to go back to page 1 of the table and to edit the header from that location. The hard copy momentarily confused the operator because the attorney did not realize that the repetitive header info is "**uneditable**" unless of course you go back to **Row 1** of the table where it originated.

4.   The operator went back to row 1 and made the changes then, went back to page 10 and continued on with the edits for the remainder of the document.

Simple, but then again, it is always simple when you have already been there.

......*

Above

Below

USING ABOVE/BELOW IN YOUR CROSS REFERENCES

In general, a cross reference (under the References Tab) keeps track of a paragraph in terms of the Multilevel Outline Number currently sitting next to the paragraph that is being referenced.

If the referenced paragraph is moved or if paragraphs are added or removed that come before the referenced paragraph, the paragraph number in the Cross Reference should automatically readjust to reflect the new position of the referenced paragraph.

1.   Sometimes the attorney will use the above/below feature in addition to the cross references. Below, a typical cross reference.

Body text body text body text See Section 2.4 Insurance Agreement for more information.

2.   Depending on where you are in the document when you reference the paragraph will determine whether it is above or below the paragraph that is doing the referencing.

3.   To use the above/below feature, first bring in your cross reference. Reference Type is "Numbered Item" and "**Insert Reference To**" should be set to "Paragraph".

See Section 2.4 Insurance Agreement for more information

4.   Place your cursor after the text of the cross reference (in this case the word "Agreement") and make sure there is at least 1 empty space.

5.   Go back into cross references, and under **"Insert Reference To"** change it to **Above/Below**.

6.   In the active listing below, choose the same paragraph number.   In this article, we would choose Section 2.4.

7.   The cross reference should read **See Section 2.4** Insurance Agreement above for more information. Note that some people place the above/below directly after the 2.4 and some place it after the entire reference as we did in this article.

8   The "**2.4**" and the word "above" should be grey if field shading is on and this cross reference will keep track of the current paragraph number next to the referenced paragraph and the position of the paragraph in relation to the paragraph that does the referencing.

……*

ADDING ATTACHMENTS TO A PDF

Most people associate PDF documents with starting out in a specific software such as MS Word and/or WorkShare output file, Excel, PowerPoint etc. and then converting those documents over to PDF. Some people like to make a neat package without uploading separate documents. I have seen it used where the PDF was instructional and then a Merge Letter and the recipient list was attached.

I came across a post where a test was given and the test taker was asked to attach both an MS Word File to a 2 page PDF as well as a .WMV file (Voicemail) file. They had 10 minutes to complete the task.

1.   You can click on the Attach Icon on the Navigation Pane or

2.   Go to the Comment Ribbon to attach the file which gives you the ability to place it anywhere in the PDF file along with a visual such as a thumbnail or paper clip.

3.   You may not use this every day but knowing this is possible, adds options that you may not have known about. The more options we have the more chances we have to solve a problem.

......*

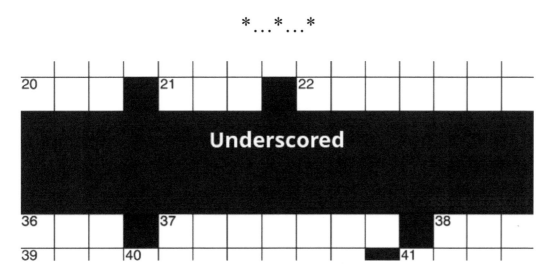

UNDERSCORE APPLIED TO PARAGRAPH

Many of you seasoned operators and secretaries will find this basic but I assure you that many people don't make the connection when doing tables.

Scenario: You have a number of headings across the top of the financial chart. Each heading is underscored or you have totals or subtotals across the page single or double underscored.

In either event, the Borders and Shading Dialog Box should be utilized to produce the underscore, but many times people (especially newer students and some operators) will associate the lines to the Cell which then causes the following:

1.   Even though the line is associated with each separate heading of each separate cell, when you view the document in Print Preview or you print out the document, the separate underscored headings will appear as one solid continuous line since this feature puts the line from end to end in the cell.

2.   People then try to remedy this by inserting narrow "**buffer columns**" that have no underscore associated with them but serve to make sure that the underscores that are beneath the Titles or Numbers are are visually separated from the underscore of the next column.

3.   While this is a remedy, it is totally unnecessary because all they needed to do was to apply the underscore or double underscore to "**Paragraph**" when underscoring Titles or Numbers in a table using Borders and Shading.

4.   By associating the underscore to "**Paragraph**" for your titles and numbers when using Borders and Shading, this feature leaves a bit of room on the left and right of each cell it is applied to. So, when you view the table or print it out, there is a clear separation between the columns and no buffer columns are necessary.

Try it yourself. It works first time and every time. If you are taking a test and you have a financial type table in the test, they will be looking for your use of applying the underscore to paragraph.

……*

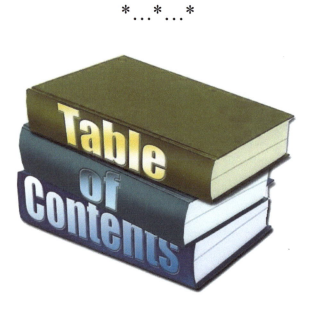

SOME OF MY TABLE OF CONTENTS ENTRIES
ARE CAPITALIZED AND SOME ARE NOT

This article will help to remove some of the mystery as to inconsistency when it comes to the look of the TOC.

Some Rules: If areas of the RAW text (the original document text) is in UPPERCASE, and you leave it in UPPERCASE, then no matter what you do in your Heading Styles will still result in your TOC entries coming in as Uppercase.

So, the usual routine is to (1) take UPPER CASE RAW Text and make it Initial Cap (Initial Cap MS Word 2003, Capitalize Each Word 2007-16). (2) Then, we build UPPERCASE into the Heading Styles that need it. When we do so, we get UPPERCASE within the document but NOT in the Table of Contents.

Character Styles also will find their way into your TOC so if you use a Character Style on text that will be part of your TOC entries such as Bold, Underscore, **ALL CAPS**, Sᴍᴀʟʟ Cᴀᴘs, those attributes will be transferred to the TOC so think twice.

So the original question was: How do I correct a Table of Contents that has a mixture of UPPER CASE and Initial Caps entries.

1.   Most TOC's are using Initial Caps. Go into the document and find the first Heading that was inadvertently carried over to the TOC in **ALL CAPS**.

2.   Strip off the Heading Style (Control Shift N).

3.   The RAW text will now be exposed. Change it to "Capitalize Each Word".

4.   Reapply the Heading Style.

5.   Re-Run your TOC after you have attended to all of the inadvertent UPPERCASE ENTRIES and the changes will take effect.

I DON'T WANT TO PRINT THE BLACK LINE CHANGES

A student of mine got a temporary position at a small legal firm. No DMS (**Document Managing System**), just a basic set-up. She opened up the first requested document to edit and it had Track Changes. She was told to leave the Track Changes On within the document but print the document out without the Track Changes.

She sent the document to print and the document has the track changes on the print out when she picked it up from the printer. When you don't know a procedure or where to go for a function or procedure, you can freeze up mentally in a work situation and not be able to resolve it. She didn't want to lose the assignment nevertheless, she had an attorney waiting on her for a "clean" printout. So how was this resolved?

In a DMS, they actually have a "Print Black Line Changes Selection" that you can select or deselect. For the small law firm that does not have a DMS we can handle this in one of two ways.

1.   Under the Review tab, choose the selection "**Final**" under the "**Display For Review**" selections. This method does not turn off the track changes but simply hides them until you switch back to "**Final Showing Markup**".

OR, WE COULD HAVE TAKEN THIS APPROACH:

2.   Under File, Print, go to File Print Settings.

3.   Under Settings, look for the Down Arrow to the right of "**Print all Pages**".

4.   Click on the Down Arrow and Uncheck "**Print Markup**".

If you choose this method, then you do not have to make any changes within the document itself such as we did in the first method in switching over to "Final".

Next time you deal with track changes or document comparison changes, please check out both methods we examined in this article for not printing the changes. Don't wait until it is an issue. Being exposed beforehand always gives you a major advantage.

......*

STRATEGICALLY USING CHARACTER STYLES

Character styles allow you to "**Style**" specific words with specific attributes such as Bolding, Underscore, Italic etc. Anything we find under the Font Menu can be applied to the Character Style.

A good example would be a scenario where we are requested to **Bold** and/ or <u>underscore</u> all the defined terms in the document. Defined Terms are the abbreviated or nickname like terms assigned to names, companies and institutions rather than referring to the name in its full form over and over again throughout the entire document. So you might see this in a typical legal document. The Securities and Exchange Commission ("Sec") ...

Other uses of Character styles take the form of changing the Font of certain company names that appear within the document. Maybe each mention of the company name is in a particular font, a particular attribute such as Bold and Italic etc.

Other documents that have Preamble like Introductions that use "**Whereas**" to start off each paragraph may be Bolding or Capitalizing the word.

This is the main point. People will sometimes use a particular character style to take care of a number of different scenarios which means that they then LOSE the ability to take care of each individual scenario without affecting the other instances that are also sharing that same character style.

1. Each individual scenario should have its own individual character style.

2. If you need to remove the attribute then modifying the style and removing it takes care of it instantly.

3. Although you remove a Character Style through modification, it is still silently marked and turning it back on through modifying takes one second.

4.   Finally, if you wish remove the character style from ONE particular instance, then highlight the instance and use "**Control Shift N**" to strip off the character style but doing so will **NOT** strip off the underlying Paragraph Style.

......*

HYPERLINKS: TABLE OF CONTENTS VS. CROSS REFERENCES

This article has to do with the functionality of the Hyperlink aspect when running a TOC vs. the Hyperlink aspect of inserting a Cross Reference. We want to examine how the Hyperlink function operates between the two separate functions.

1.   When we run a Table of Contents and we make the choice of "Use Hyperlink Instead of Page Numbers" this covers us for those scenarios where "Web Preview" is going to be utilized. Instead of Page Numbers, the TOC entries themselves become the Hyperlinks. So, if this is published to the Web, the TOC entries will be links.

2.   When not in "Web Preview", you can make use of the Hyperlink function by taking your cursor over to the Page Number and use Control + Click. It should be noted that whether you choose the Hyperlink function or not, you will always have the option to Control + Click on the page numbers of the completed TOC to be taken to any particular Heading of the document.

3.   As to cross references, when you choose Hyperlink before you choose the section to Cross Reference in the Cross Section Dialog box, this will ensure that when the Cross Reference comes in within the document, you can make use of Control + Click to jump to the Cross Referenced item.

4.   If you DO NOT select the Hyperlink box before selecting the cross referenced item, when the Cross Reference comes in within the document, you will NOT have the ability to Control + Click on the Cross Reference in order to be hopped to the referenced paragraph.

5. The Cross Reference will update as it should but many people like the ability to hop to a referenced paragraph as needed. So, in the TOC of a law firm setting Hyperlinks are not that crucial but in terms of the Cross Reference it is a vital and expected aspect of this particular function.

......*

ALERTNESS, ROUTINES AND FOCUS HELP TO AVOID MISTAKES AND TO SOLVE MS WORD PROBLEMS

It was a simple thing under File-Options/Display/"**Printing Options**" and an unchecked box called "Print drawings created in Word"

The word "**Drawings**" threw me off but it was the reason why my Text Box was not printing. Making mental note of things that are not intuitive in MS Word goes a long way.

Did you know that Insert File is under "Objects"? Sometimes things just don't appear where you expect them to.

In talking further about attention to detail. I have seen the following scenario unfold numerous times and this situation will help to underscore the importance of an established routine.

Scenario: Attorney brings down a document. He says: Dupe the document and make the heavy markup changes under a new document number. Do NOT touch the original document.

1. Operator dupes document. He writes the new document number on his log sheet while he is in the process of filling out the document summary.

2. What the operator does not realize is that the footer did not update properly from the DMS (Document Management System) and the new document is still displaying the "original" document number in the footer.

3. He goes directly into the new file and after doing about 5 pages of heavy edits he places a pickup sheet telling the next operator where to continue the edits.

4.   As most operators do, they pick up the mark-up, look at the footer and go into the document number on the bottom of the page whereupon they continue the editing in the original file and not the new file. He finishes the file, prints it out and sends it back to the attorney.

5.   The attorney receives a document that he asked not to be edited "edited" and the first five pages of the new document being done properly but the attorney has no clue it even exists. It will be up to a confused coordinator and the original operator to finally figure out what happened here. This is a mess and could have been totally been avoided if the operator simply checked the new file to make sure the footer updated. Small routines such as checking the footer go a long way.

Routines and double checking what you do will give you the assurance that each job goes smoothly.

BLOCKING BLUE LIGHT SPECTRUM STEMMING FROM
TV, COMPUTERS AND SMART PHONES.

As you may know, melatonin lowers in the daytime and increases in the evening which helps you to feel sleepy.

Artificial light that stems from TV, Cell Phones and Computers suppress Melatonin and in sensitive people it can cause problems in going to sleep.

Here are a few ideas to suppress artificial light (Blue Light Spectrum)

1.   Download https://justgetflux.com. Free download for your computer or iPhone

2.   For Computer Screens and TV Screens.

https://www.lowbluelights.com/products.asp

3.   Blue Blocker Sun Glasses

......*

RESETTING YOUR KEYBOARD BACK TO ITS ORIGINAL SETTINGS

SCENARIO:

This will help whether you are at work or at home. So you sit down at a work station and when you use a standard shortcut key such as Control R (align right) and it gives you something else other than what was expected. So in this case instead of aligning a piece of text to the extreme right of the screen, it pastes in a signature block.

Most of the time this is due to people doing a Macro and using a standard shortcut key combination to activate their macro.

When doing Macros, you really want to use a key combination that does not **"interfere"** with the existing well known short cut key combinations.

Nevertheless, in some cases you end up in a situation where the PC is not operating in a recognizable fashion due to someone re-assigning well known short-cut keys to other procedures. The question becomes how do we set the keyboard back to the original settings so the PC reacts in a way we are used to.

1.   Display the Word Options dialog box. (In Word 2007 click the Office button and then click Word Options. In Word 2010-13 display the File tab of the ribbon and then click Options.)

2.   At the left of the dialog box click Customize.

Click the Customize button (Word 2007) or the Customize Ribbon button (Word 2010-13).

3.   Word displays the Customize Keyboard dialog box.

Click on the Reset All button. (NOTE: This button is only available if you've previously made customizations to the keyboard shortcuts.)

4.   Word displays a dialog box asking if you want to remove all your shortcut key definitions.

Click on Yes. Word removes all the user-defined shortcut keys, returning them to their default condition.

Click on Close to back out of the Customize Keyboard dialog box.

Click on Cancel to back out of the Word Options dialog box.

*It should be noted that in smaller firms, multiple people using the same workstation can experience the above. You may wish to relegate one particular workstation that makes use of the **unorthodox keyboard shortcuts** so you don't affect other users.

The question in larger firms that make use of individual log-ins, resulting in individual desktops that appear on the screen as a result of a particular log-in is how they react to the changing of keyboard shortcuts.

Depending on how the firm sets up their system, if one user changes his/her keyboard shortcuts and then logs out the new user who logs in may not experience those changes. But the opposite can be true as well meaning someone logs in, changes some of the generic keyboard shortcuts which take effect on the local hard drive of that particular workstation and are then experienced by the next user to log in at that particular workstation.

The next time you use a short cut key and you receive a something totally unexpected instead, you will now know how to restore your keyboard back to its recognizable form.

......*

**OMITTING THE DOTTED LEADER AND PAGE NUMBER
FROM HEADING 1 OF YOUR TOC.**

This scenario is for a **Centered Level TOC 1** without the **dotted leader** and page number. This makes use of what is called Switches within the **TOC Field Code**.

Without getting deep into the use of switches, this short article will give you the info you need if you are asked to omit the dotted leader and page number from the first level of your TOC (Heading 1). In this scenario, the TOC is usually centered but it can be left aligned as well. So, here we go:

1.   The first thing to do in order to change the TOC so Level 1 comes in without the Dotted Leader and Page Number is to Modify TOC 1 and make it centered. If the hard copy is not centered then go right to Step 2.

2.   Collapse the TOC into a Field Code by doing Shift F9. Shift F9 also toggles the TOC back to its full form. If the entire TOC does not collapse to one line of code then highlight the entire field of the TOC and then do Shift F9 and that will collapse it for sure.

3.   When you collapse down the TOC into a Field Code, replace the current Field Code Contents with what you see below. Type in exactly what you see below into your current Field Code.

{ TOC \o "1-2" \n 1-1 }

4.   Rerun your TOC and the Dotted Leader and Page Number will be gone.

......*

PROBLEM IN DOCUMENT HIDING IN PLAIN SIGHT

As in many articles that I have authored, here is another scenario you would like to have been exposed to before it happens in a live situation.

Scenario: My student has a test at an employment agency for a Word Processing Operator position. She works on an older MAC using MS Word 2010 at home which doesn't allow her to do the Style Separator feature. So, she resorts to using the old "**Hidden Paragraph**" method in order to be able to run a TOC without the entire Body Text Portion of the Heading 2 paragraph ending up in the TOC.

1.   In this same document, she needs to mark the document for Index of Terms, Table of Authorities and Cross References.

2.   Upon highlighting her 1st "Defined Term" the area in the Dialog box that allows one to complete the marking process was Grayed Out. The same situation occurred when attempting to mark a Table of Authority Entry and a Cross Reference Entry.

3.   Looking at the Body Text Portion of her Heading 2 Paragraph, she had properly named it "**Remainder of Para**" which served to disassociate the Body Text Portion of the Heading 2 paragraph ensuring her TOC would run properly.

4.   What I did notice was on that Body Text Paragraph, it had the Tell Tale Dotted Line under the entire length of the paragraph. This means that the paragraph has the "**Hidden**" attribute within the makeup of the style itself. I know it is in the style simply because ALL of the Heading 2 body text portions have the dotted lines and not just ONE occurrence.

5.   Modifying the style and removing "Hidden" under Font, solves the problem of not allowing one the ability to mark the Index of Terms, TOA and Cross References.

6.   Using the old Hidden Method in place of the Style Separator requires that you only mark the paragraph symbol that follows the Heading 2 "**heading text**" as "**Hidden**" . Yes, you place a Hard Return after your Heading 2 Heading Text and apply the **Hidden** Attribute to it.

......*

HAVING A NUMBER OF OPTIONS WHEN USING THE ZOOM FEATURE...

As you know, if you are working in a big firm, most probably all of your work station settings are tied into your log-on. No one else but you changes anything.

But, for some of you, this is not the case. You sit down at a work station possibly as a temporary employee or you share a work station and you are the recipient of whatever is going on at that particular work station.

If you are a secretary or word processing operator, there are times when an attorney will stand right over you to direct last minute editing changes. You don't want to be in a position where you don't have access to your zoom feature. It is very common for the attorney or other individual to ask that you enlarge the text so they can read it without straining. Below are some options:

1.   If you find that the Zoom and Zoom Slider which are vital are not present on the bottom right of your screen above your status bar, you simply right click on your status bar and place a check next to "**Zoom**" (which shows your viewing percentage) and "**Zoom Slider**" that allows you to enlarge and shrink the screen size. You find these at the bottom of the list. Those two are most commonly used.

2.   Under the View Tab, you can get to the **Zoom** feature, but certainly not as convenient as having it active on the screen.

3.   If you have a roller on the top of your mouse, you can use **Control + Roll Forward or Backward** to shrink or enlarge the text. This is easy and requires no turning on/off specific features on the Status Bar Menu.

Now you have some options when it comes to your Zoom feature.

......*

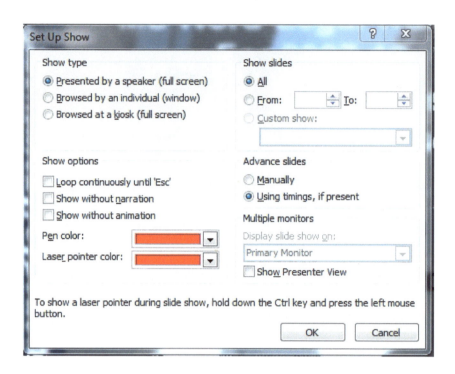

USING THE INTERNAL LASER POINTER DURING
A POWER POINT SLIDE SHOW

This is a fun little Tid-Bit

This is very easy to Use:

SCENARIO:

You are running a Power Point Slide Show and while you are running the Slide Show for your audience, you want to make use of Power Point's internal Laser Pointer.

1. Under the "**Slide Show**" tab, go to the "Set Up Slide Show Button".

2. When you are in the "**Set Up Slide Show Button**" dialog box, set your "Laser Pointer Color". Most people from my experience choose red.

3. When you run the slide show, use your **Control** and **Left Mouse Button** to point things out to your audience using the internal laser.

4. That is all you need to do.....

......*

OH NO, MY TABLE OF CONTENTS LEVELS ARE NOT INDENTING...

From time to time, you run a Table of Contents and for no apparent reason, the levels of the TOC are not indenting. There are a number of reasons why this occurs.

1.   The settings for that particular document shell have been set to zero for TOC 1-9 or part of 1-9 for whatever reason. There are other problems relating to switches.

2.   The problem is that we almost always find out about this problem after we run the TOC so it is after the fact.

3.   If you know the following settings you can correct this scenario right away.

4.   In the default TOC styles, TOC 2 through 9 are indented by 11 points from the level before. The settings that control the Indentations are found under Format, Paragraph Left Indent so if you use inch units the indents from TOC 2 forward will be **0.15", 0.31", 0.46", 0.61",** etc.)

5.   Sometimes you will need to readjust a Tab Setting as well as the your Left Margin.

6.   To modify the TOC Styles you can (In **Draft View**) Double Click On the TOC style in your Style Area Tracking (Left Side) which will bring up your Modify Box. You. can also bring up the Apply Style Toolbar (**Control Shift S**) and search out your TOC style that you need to modify from the window at the top.

Make your changes to the proper TOC level and your Table of Contents should be fine.

......*

PAY ATTENTION TO WHERE YOUR CURSOR IS...

SCENARIO:

Heading 2

Section 2.01 The Contract (Style Separator) (a) (List Num Field Code) Body Text Body Text Body Text Body Text Body Text Body Text Body Text Body Text Body Text Body Text.

Heading 3

(b). Text Text Text Text Text Text Text Text Text Text Text Text Text Text Text Text Text Text Text Text Text Text.

1.   Above we have a situation whereby **Heading 2** shares the paragraph, so a Style Separator is used in order to signify where the **Heading 2** text ends for purposes of generating your TOC.

2.   After the Style Separator, you have an **"(a)"** within the paragraph starting at the beginning of the Body Text portion of Heading 2. This **"(a)"** is making use of the "Listnum Field Code" and forces Heading Level 3 over to **(b)** as shown in the example above.

WHAT IS THE POINT?

3.   Not knowing how to insert the ListNum Field Code, the operator went into the Multilevel Dialog Box and instructed **Heading 3** to "**Start At B**" for that section of text.

4.   When informed that the ListNum Field Code "should" be used in place of Heading 3 starting at "**B**", the operator attempted to get back into the Multilevel Dialog box to change Heading 3 to say Start at "**A**" . When entering the Dialog Box, the "**Start At**" selection was grayed out and could not be accessed.

5.   The operator had the cursor sitting in the Body Text portion of Heading 2 causing the disabling (graying out) of the "**Start At**" area.

6.   The operator changed the location of the cursor to the Heading 3 area and when entering the Multilevel Dialog Box the "Start At" selection was now available. The Start At section was now changed to **Start At "A"** and when the ListNum Field Code was inserted in the Heading 2 paragraph that I showed you above, the Heading 3 below naturally and properly kicked over to (b).

The proper positioning of your cursor ensures that all features of the Multilevel Dialog Box are active.

......*

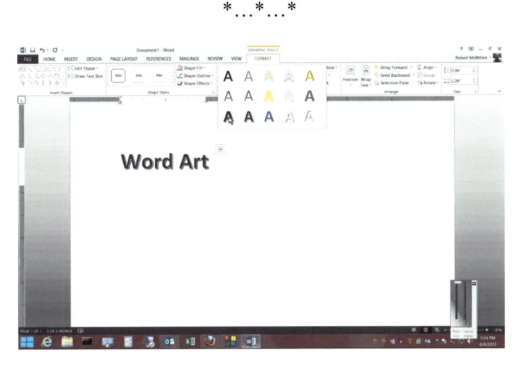

REMOVING WORD ART STYLES FROM TEXT IN POWERPOINT

Since 2007 MS PowerPoint has improved the Word Art Styles (under Drawing Tools) that give you a lot more choices that can quickly be applied to text. You also get to "**try on**" each look by simply placing your cursor over the particular color scheme that catches you eye. It then will show you the look as you go from color to color. In this way, you don't have to apply anything until you find what you want.

It is not quickly apparent how to remove the attribute altogether if you decide you want the Word Art Style to be taken off that piece of text.

This can save you a lot of valuable time if you need to have it removed.

To remove the no longer wanted Word Art:

1.   Highlight the text that has the Word Art you wish to remove.

2.   Go to your Home Tab.

3.   In your Font area (to the right of "Decrease Font" and to the left of your "Bullets" button) look for a double Aa with a small Eraser.

4.   That is your "**Clear Formatting**" button. Click it and that will remove the effect. You can also highlight the text and use **Control Space** to achieve the same result.

Every little bit of knowledge will help at one point or another.

......*

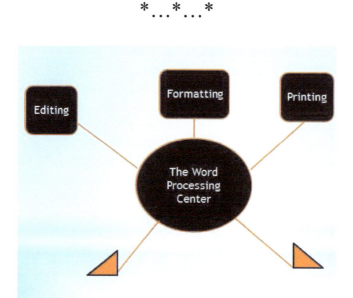

GROUPING CHARTS THAT ARE PUT TOGETHER FROM SCRATCH

This article deals with PowerPoint Charts that were **NOT** created with the SmartArt Pre-Set Chart Selections.

Sometimes, people will construct charts from scratch and another operator will inherit that chart to edit it. An item that comes up again and again is the subject of Grouping.

1.   When a chart is totally "**ungrouped**", the separate pieces (lines, boxes, arrows, ovals etc.) are independently controllable in terms of moving around on the slide.

2.   When a chart is grouped, either partially or totally, the piece that is "grouped" can be copied, shifted **up-down-left-right** by tugging or use of **Control (North-South-East-West)** for Micro Moving. You are now in a position to control the entire chart or a piece of a chart instead of moving each piece of the chart independently to adjust the charts position on the slide. Charts can have many pieces to deal with so this can be very time consuming.

3.   To grab the entire chart in order to "Group" it, **click** on one of the objects in the chart such as a box or oval and then use "**Control A**" which highlights all the pieces of the chart. Click on the "**Drawing Tools**" Tab (upper right) and select "**Group**". The chart will now respond as one solid piece to be moved around as needed.

4.   When you grab your chart to group it by use of "**Control A**", you will also grab footer material on the slide such as **Date**, **Page No**. etc. since the pieces of the footer are using "text boxes".   To **de-select** the footer material, or for that matter **ANY MATERIAL** that you do not want in the grouping do the following: Go over to the object and "**Shift Click**". Once you have **de-selected** the pieces that you don't want in the group go to **Drawing Tools** and group the remaining selected pieces.

5.   You can also grab the pieces of the chart by **sweeping your cursor** over the area to be grouped and when you let go, the piece that you highlighed will show all of the pieces now selected. Then you can go to **Drawing Tools** and select "**Group**".

6.   Finally, if you wish to group the chart and copy it to another slide you group the pieces of the chart that you need, click on the grouped piece and select copy (Control C). Now you can go to the slide that needs the grouped piece and paste it in using Control V.

CONCLUSION

We have reached the end of book number 4! You now have more insight and knowledge than before you read this book. Whether you are a secretary or word processing operator, this information will be very valuable for you. In fact, many of the scenarios that I covered in the four volumes will come up at work for sure. The advantage is that because I was able to expose the scenarios to you, they will not seem so foreign to you and you will have a quicker response and solution,

Please feel free to keep in touch with me. You can always reach me at 888-422-0692 Ext.2 or email at louis@advanceto.com or louisellman@gmail.com.

All the best!

Louis

BONUS

**CROWDING OF THE NUMBER SYSTEM| ON THE TABLE OF CONTENTS
OR TABLE OF AUTHORITIES AS WELL AS PROPER FONT
FOR HEADINGS WITHIN TOC AND TOA**

By Louis Ellman

Table Heading	············"··············Page Break···············
	Table·of·Contents¶
Page No. TOA	Page¶
TOA Heading	**Cases¶**
Table of Authoritie	Am.·Trade·Partners·v.·A-1·Int'l·Importing·Enterprises,·Ltd.,·757·F.·Supp.·545·(E.D.·Pa.·1991)→.4¶
Table of Authoritie	Anderson·v.·Pine·South·Capital,·LLC,·177·F.·Supp.·2d·591 .... → 7¶
Table of Authoritie	Bank·of·Vermont·v.·Lyndonville·Sav.·Bank·&·Trust·Co.,·906·F.·Supp.·221,·227·(D.·Vt.·1995)→.6¶
Table of Authoritie	In·re·Credit·Acceptance·Corp.·Secs.·Lit.,·50·F.·Supp.·2d·662,·671·(E.D.·Mich.·1999) → .8¶
Table of Authoritie	Learjet·Corp.·v.·Spenlinhauer,·901·F.2d·198·(1st·Cir.·1990)·(same);·Peerless·Mills,·Inc.·v.· AT&T,·527·F.2d·445·(2d·Cir.·1975) → 9¶
Table of Authoritie	Michaels·Bldg.·Co.·v.·Ameritrust·Co.,·N.A.,·848·F.2d·674·(6th·Cir.·1988)). → 8¶
Table of Authoritie	Picard·Chem.·Inc.·Profit·Sharing·Plan·v.·Perrigo·Co.,·940·F.·Supp.·1101·(W.D.·Mich.·1996) →.7¶
Table of Authoritie	Reves·v.·Ernst,·507·U.S.·170,·185·(1993) .... → 6¶
Table of Authoritie	Rolo·v.·City·Investing·Co.·Liquidating·Trust,·845·F.·Supp.·182,·233-34·(D.N.J.·1993) ......→ 6¶
Table of Authoritie	See·Brouwer·v.·Raffensperger·Hughes·&·Co.,·199·F.3d·961,·967·(7th·Cir.). → 5¶
Table of Authoritie	See·Cincinnati·Ins.·Co.·v.·Hertz·Corp.,·776·F.·Supp.·1235,·1238·(S.D.·Ohio·1991) ....→........2¶
Table of Authoritie	See·e.g.,·Van·Dorn·Co.·v.·Howington,·623·F.·Supp.·1548,·1555·(N.D.·Ohio·1995) ....→........3¶
Table of Authoritie	See·Michaels·Bldg.·Co.·v.·Ameritrust·Co.,·N.A.,·848·F.2d·674·(6th·Cir.·1988)..............→.........7¶
Normal	¶

SAMPLE

1.   There are **two issues** here that I want to examine and take care of with you. If you look at the sample Table of Authorities above, and you look at the Heading (**Cases**) with a style associated with it of "**TOA Heading**" you will notice that the individual **Cases** listed in the TOA are in **Times New Roman 12** while the **TOA Heading is not**. It happens to be in **Ariel 12** which is a common quirk of the system. Most operators don't even notice it and routinely hand in work where the font of the TOA Headings is in Ariel. Eventually, it gets noticed by the attorney and they ask the operator to fix it. You should be aware of this MS Word problem before hand. So, in order to fix the TOA Heading you can either **Double click** on the **TOA Heading style listed on the left hand side** or **right click** on the TOA Heading style within the **Style and Formatting Panel** on the **Right hand side**. If you place your cursor **on the "Cases" Line** the TOA Heading style name will appear in the top window of the **side Panel**. I will use that side panel method to correct the style. Right Click on **TOA Heading**..

Formatting of selected text

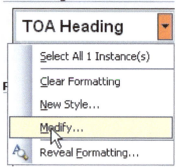

2.   Under Modify, change the Font over to **Times New Roman.** If you do it through **Modify**, then the fix is **permanent**. If you do it through **direct formatting**, then every time that someone runs the Table of Authorities (**Updates it**) it will simply go back to **the way it was** before it was fixed since it was **not corrected within the actual style** but **on the surface** due to **direct formatting**.

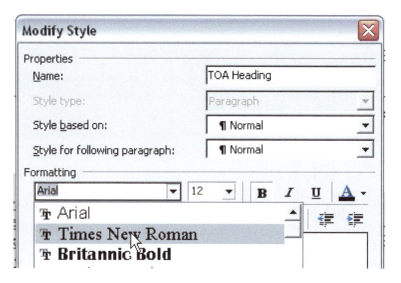

Table Heading	" —————————————Page Break————————————
	Table·of·Contents¶
Page No. TOA	Page¶
TOA Heading	**Cases¶**
Table of Authoritie	Am.·Trade·Partners·v.·A-1·Int'l·Importing·Enterprises,·Ltd.,·757·F.·Supp.·545·(E.D.·Pa·1991)→4¶
Table of Authoritie	Anderson·v.·Pine·South·Capital,·LLC,·177·F.·Supp.·2d·591 →7¶
Table of Authoritie	Bank·of·Vermont·v.·Lyndonville·Sav.·Bank·&·Trust·Co.,·906·F.·Supp.·221,·227·(D.·Vt.·1995)→6¶
Table of Authoritie	In·re·Credit·Acceptance·Corp.·Secs.·Lit.,·50·F.·Supp.·2d·662,·671·(E.D.·Mich.·1999) ....→........8¶
Table of Authoritie	Learjet·Corp.·v.·Spenlinhauer,·901·F.2d·198·(1st·Cir.·1990)·(same);·Peerless·Mills,·Inc.·v.·
	AT&T,·527·F.2d·445·(2d·Cir.·1975) ....→.............9¶
Table of Authoritie	Michaels·Bldg.·Co.·v.·Ameritrust·Co.,·N.A.,·848·F.2d·674·(6th·Cir.·1988)...........→.......8¶
Table of Authoritie	Picard·Chem.·Inc.·Profit·Sharing·Plan·v.·Perrigo·Co.,·940·F.·Supp.·1101·(W.D.·Mich.·1996)·→.7¶
Table of Authoritie	Reves·v.·Ernst,·507·U.S.·170,·185·(1993) ....→.............6¶
Table of Authoritie	Rolo·v.·City·Investing·Co.·Liquidating·Trust,·845·F.·Supp.·182,·233-34·(D.N.J.·1993) ....→......6¶
Table of Authoritie	See·Brouwer·v.·Raffensperger·Hughes·&·Co.,·199·F.3d·961,·967·(7th·Cir.) ....→........5¶
Table of Authoritie	See·Cincinnati·Ins.·Co.·v.·Hertz·Corp.,·776·F.·Supp.·1235,·1238·(S.D.·Ohio·1991) ....→....2¶
Table of Authoritie	See·e.g.,·Van·Dorn·Co.·v.·Howington,·623·F.·Supp.·1548,·1555·(N.D.·Ohio·1995) ....→....3¶
Table of Authoritie	See·Michaels·Bldg.·Co.·v.·Ameritrust·Co.,·N.A.,·848·F.2d·674·(6th·Cir.·1988)............→....7¶
Normal	¶

3.   Take a look at the TOA sample above again. Now I want to focus on the text that is **crowding the page numbers to the extreme right**. There are a couple of areas in the TOA where the closed **Parenthesis of the Year of the case gets awfully close** to the **page numbers**. Sometimes an attorney will notice it and ask the operator to please **tidy it up** meaning to get the text away from the page numbers to the right so that it does not look so **cluttered**. Many people do not know how to do this properly so they **manually go to the ruler and fix it like that**. But, each time that the TOA is updated **the problem resurfaces** since it was done with direct formatting. So, the question becomes **what controls the text of the completed TOA** so that we can improve the look of the TOA and it will be fixed once and for all.

Table Heading	" —————————————Page Break————————————
	Table·of·Contents¶
Page No. TOA	Page¶
TOA Heading	**Cases¶**
Table of Authoritie	Am.·Trade·Partners·v.·A-1·Int'l·Importing·Enterprises,·Ltd.,·757·F.·Supp.·545·(E.D.·Pa·1991)→4¶
Table of Authoritie	Anderson·v.·Pine·South·Capital,·LLC,·177·F.·Supp.·2d·591 ....→.........7¶
Table of Authoritie	Bank·of·Vermont·v.·Lyndonville·Sav.·Bank·&·Trust·Co.,·906·F.·Supp.·221,·227·(D.·Vt.·1995)→6¶
Table of Authoritie	In·re·Credit·Acceptance·Corp.·Secs.·Lit.,·50·F.·Supp.·2d·662,·671·(E.D.·Mich.·1999) ....→........8¶
Table of Authoritie	Learjet·Corp.·v.·Spenlinhauer,·901·F.2d·198·(1st·Cir.·1990)·(same);·Peerless·Mills,·Inc.·v.·
	AT&T,·527·F.2d·445·(2d·Cir.·1975) ....→.............9¶
Table of Authoritie	Michaels·Bldg.·Co.·v.·Ameritrust·Co.,·N.A.,·848·F.2d·674·(6th·Cir.·1988)...........→.......8¶
Table of Authoritie	Picard·Chem.·Inc.·Profit·Sharing·Plan·v.·Perrigo·Co.,·940·F.·Supp.·1101·(W.D.·Mich.·1996)·→.7¶
Table of Authoritie	Reves·v.·Ernst,·507·U.S.·170,·185·(1993) ....→.............6¶
Table of Authoritie	Rolo·v.·City·Investing·Co.·Liquidating·Trust,·845·F.·Supp.·182,·233-34·(D.N.J.·1993) ....→......6¶
Table of Authoritie	See·Brouwer·v.·Raffensperger·Hughes·&·Co.,·199·F.3d·961,·967·(7th·Cir.) ....→........5¶
Table of Authoritie	See·Cincinnati·Ins.·Co.·v.·Hertz·Corp.,·776·F.·Supp.·1235,·1238·(S.D.·Ohio·1991) ....→....2¶
Table of Authoritie	See·e.g.,·Van·Dorn·Co.·v.·Howington,·623·F.·Supp.·1548,·1555·(N.D.·Ohio·1995) ....→....3¶
Table of Authoritie	See·Michaels·Bldg.·Co.·v.·Ameritrust·Co.,·N.A.,·848·F.2d·674·(6th·Cir.·1988)............→....7¶
Normal	¶

4. Look at the left hand side of the sample above. The style associated with the completed TOA entries is called "Table of Authorities". I want you to do the following:

Either **double click** on the left hand side style (when in **Draft View**) "Table of Authorities" or right click on the right hand side panel on the style "**Table of Authorities**".

Under **Modify**, go to **Format Paragraph** and under **Indentation "Right"** make that 0.5. That will take all of the text of the Table of Authorities and will **push it back** towards the left an additional **0.5** thus making a **clear lane** between the **Table of Authorities** Text and the **Page Numbering**.

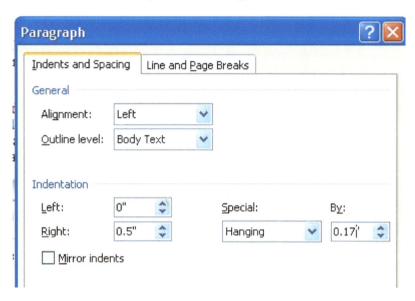

5. If you look at the ruler when your cursor is in the TOA you will notice that there is a **right tab in the ruler** toward the extreme right. **YOU DO NOT TOUCH THAT!** The right tab on the ruler in the TOC and TOA ▂ controls t**he actual Page numbering** all the way to the right.

6 Finally it is very important to note that if your TOC has this same problem, where text is crowding the page numbering that you will go about fixing it in the same manner by modifying either **TOC 1** or **TOC 2 or both if necessary**. Below is **the corrected TOA** for you to see the difference:

www.ingramcontent.com/pod-product-compliance
Lightning Source LLC
LaVergne TN
LVHW071523070326
832902LV00002B/51